THE POETRY OF BARIUM

The Poetry of Barium

Walter the Educator

SKB

Silent King Books a WhichHead Imprint

Copyright © 2023 by Walter the Educator

All rights reserved. No part of this book may be reproduced in any manner whatsoever without written permission except in the case of brief quotations embodied in critical articles and reviews.

First Printing, 2023

"Earning a degree in chemistry changed my life!"
– Walter the Educator

dedicated to all the chemistry lovers, like myself, across the world

CONTENTS

Dedication v

Why I Created This Book? 1

One - Barium, The Beauty Of The Land . . . 2

Two - Symbol Of Discovery 4

Three - Barium, The Star 6

Four - Center Stage 8

Five - Versatile Element 10

Six - Barium, The Element 12

Seven - Forever To Remain 14

Eight - Igniting A Spark 16

Nine - For All To See 18

Ten - Fire And Art 20

Eleven - Never Tires 22

Twelve - A True Marvel 24

Thirteen - Unlock 26

Fourteen - No One Behind 28

Fifteen - Enchanting 30

Sixteen - Shines 32

Seventeen - Standing Tall 34

Eighteen - Barium, Oh Barium 36

Nineteen - Reign 38

Twenty - Catalyst Of Wonder 40

Twenty-One - Fond 42

Twenty-Two - Symphony Of Elements . . . 44

Twenty-Three - Possibility Begins 46

Twenty-Four - Your Story 48

Twenty-Five - Brings Us Light 50

Twenty-Six - Cosmic Space 52

Twenty-Seven - Barium, You're A Wonder . . 54

Twenty-Eight - In Awe 56

Twenty-Nine - A Treasure 58

Thirty - The Luminescent Gem 60

Thirty-One - Untold 62

Thirty-Two - Darkest Night 64

Thirty-Three - Every Embrace	. . . .	66
Thirty-Four - With You, Barium	. . . .	68
About The Author	. . . .	70

WHY I CREATED THIS BOOK?

Creating a poetry book about the chemical element Barium was an intriguing endeavor. Barium, with its atomic number 56 and symbol Ba, possesses various characteristics that can serve as metaphors or themes for poetic exploration. Its properties, such as its reactivity, luminescence, and the role it plays in medical imaging, can be utilized to convey emotions, explore scientific concepts, or even delve into deeper philosophical or existential themes. By blending art and science, this poetry book centered around Barium can offer a fresh perspective and provide a bridge between seemingly disparate fields.

ONE

BARIUM, THE BEAUTY OF THE LAND

In the depths of Earth where secrets lie,
A metal waits, with a gleam in its eye.
Barium, the element, so pure and bright,
A radiant star in the darkest night.

A silvery-white, lustrous treasure,
With properties that bring both joy and pleasure.
It dances with flames, a vibrant hue,
Igniting the skies with a sizzling debut.

Its atomic number, fifty-six,
A symbol of strength, a chemistry mix.
Within its core, electrons spin,
Creating a bond, a cosmic kin.

Barium, the conductor of light,
In the lab, it shines so bright.

It paints the flames in emerald green,
A spectacle, a sight unseen.

In medicine, it plays a crucial role,
As barium sulfate, it fills the bowl.
A contrast agent, it helps us see,
The inner workings of humanity.

From fireworks to glass, it finds its way,
Barium, a versatile element they say.
With a touch of magic, it brings delight,
An alchemist's dream, a brilliant light.

So let us celebrate this element grand,
Barium, the beauty of the land.
With its atomic weight, it holds the key,
To a world of wonders, for all to see.

TWO

SYMBOL OF DISCOVERY

In the realm of the elements, a radiant gem I find,
Barium, the conductor of light, a treasure so divine.
With an atomic number of fifty-six, it claims its rightful place,
A versatile element, adorned with grace.

Oh, Barium, thou dost ignite a vibrant flame,
A spectacle of colors, a pyrotechnic game.
In fireworks and flares, thy brilliance shines so bright,
A mesmerizing dance, a captivating sight.

But beyond the realm of sparks and fiery display,
Barium, thou art revered in a different way.
In the realm of medicine, thou dost play a part,
As a contrast agent, revealing secrets of the heart.

Through veins and vessels, thou dost gracefully flow,

Unveiling hidden paths, where mysteries lie below.
Thy radiance illuminates, unveiling truths unknown,
A beacon of clarity, in realms of flesh and bone.

    Barium, thou art a source of joy and wonder,
A conductor of light, a spectacle to ponder.
In thy presence, beauty and science intertwine,
A testament to the mysteries of our design.

    So, let us celebrate Barium, this element divine,
A versatile gem, with powers so fine.
In flames and medicine, its glory shall endure,
A symbol of discovery, forever pure.

THREE

BARIUM, THE STAR

In the realm of elements, Barium does shine,
A radiant presence, both pure and divine.
With an atomic number of fifty-six,
Its beauty and brilliance, a mesmerizing mix.

In the world of pyrotechnics, it takes center stage,
Igniting the heavens with its vibrant blaze.
As fireworks burst, illuminating the night,
Barium's golden glow fills hearts with delight.

But beyond the spectacle, a secret it holds,
A contrast agent in medicine, its story unfolds.
In X-rays and scans, it helps us see clear,
Barium's magic, making images appear.

As the light passes through, it conducts with grace,
Its electrons dancing, a captivating embrace.

From the crimson hues to the deepest blues,
Barium's luminescence, a magical muse.
 In the laboratory, scientists explore,
Unlocking its mysteries, forever more.
Its compounds and reactions, a scientific delight,
Barium's properties, a captivating sight.
 So let us celebrate this versatile element,
For its radiance and beauty, so ever-present.
From fireworks to medicine, it plays its part,
Barium, the star that shines in every heart.

FOUR

CENTER STAGE

In the realm of elements, there lies a radiant star,
Barium, versatile and splendid, shining from afar.
A vibrant luminescence, a beauty to behold,
Its story etched in fireworks, and tales yet untold.

In pyrotechnic dances, it paints the midnight sky,
A mesmerizing spectacle, where dreams and wonders lie.
With hues of green and blue, it lights up the night,
Barium's dazzling flare, a celestial delight.

But beyond the spectacle, in the realm of science's stride,
Barium serves a purpose, as a contrast deep inside.
Within the human vessel, it finds its second home,
A contrast agent, guiding physicians as they roam.

Through vessels and organs, it weaves its wondrous

trail,
Aiding in the diagnosis, where mysteries unveil.
A beacon in the darkness, it reveals the hidden truth,
Barium's gentle touch, a testament to its youth.

So let us raise our voices, in praise of Barium's might,
A luminescent element, that dazzles day and night.
From fireworks to medicine, it casts its spell with grace,
Barium, the radiant star, forever taking center stage.

FIVE

VERSATILE ELEMENT

In the depths of the Earth's embrace,
A hidden gem, a soft trace,
Barium, a name that whispers grace,
A chemical element with a glowing face.

With atomic number fifty-six,
It dances through the periodic mix,
A metal, heavy, yet quick,
Barium, a beauty you can't resist.

In fiery nights, it takes its flight,
Igniting the skies with colors so bright,
A pyrotechnic spectacle, a dazzling sight,
Barium, the star of the night.

But beyond the fireworks, it finds its place,
In medicine, a healing embrace,

As a contrast agent, it leaves no trace,
Barium, a guardian of grace.
    From X-rays to CT scans,
It reveals the secrets, the inner plans,
Guiding doctors with steady hands,
Barium, a light in medical lands.
    So let us celebrate this element divine,
Its luminescence, its power to shine,
Barium, a symbol of brilliance and design,
A versatile element, forever enshrined.

SIX

BARIUM, THE ELEMENT

In the realm of elements, a star does shine,
Barium, the luminescent divine.
With atomic number fifty-six,
Its properties, a scientific mix.

    A silvery-white metal, so pure and bright,
Barium dances with electrifying might.
Soft and malleable, it takes its form,
In compounds and alloys, its beauty is born.

    In medicine, Barium plays a vital role,
A contrast agent, a diagnostic goal.
From X-rays to scans, it aids the way,
Revealing secrets that the body may convey.

    But beyond the realms of science and health,
Barium ignites the night with vibrant stealth.

In fireworks, it dazzles, colors ablaze,
A symphony of light, an enchanting craze.
   So, let us celebrate this element grand,
With sparks of wonder, it takes its stand.
From laboratories to the darkened skies,
Barium, the element that never dies.

SEVEN

FOREVER TO REMAIN

In the realm of elements, let Barium shine,
A luminescent presence, so truly divine.
With atomic number fifty-six, it stands,
A symbol of brilliance in nature's grand plans.

Barium, oh Barium, a contrast so bright,
A beacon of hope in diagnostic light.
As a contrast agent, it reveals hidden truths,
Unveiling the secrets that lie within you.

In medicine's realm, it plays a vital role,
Enhancing imaging, a story to unfold.
Through X-rays and scans, it paints a clear view,
Guiding the path to a diagnosis that's true.

But Barium's wonders don't end in the lab,
For in fireworks, it dazzles, a sight to grab.

With vibrant greens and vivid embers of red,
It dances in the sky, filling hearts with widespread.
    Explosions of color, a symphony of light,
Barium's magic, a spectacle so bright.
From the darkness it emerges, a celestial art,
Captivating the night, igniting every heart.
    So let us celebrate Barium, this radiant star,
A substance of wonder, both near and far.
In medicine and fireworks, it holds its reign,
A symbol of brilliance, forever to remain.

EIGHT

IGNITING A SPARK

In the realm of science, Barium does shine,
A contrast agent, revealing secrets divine.
Through veins and vessels, it gracefully glides,
Unveiling truths hidden, where darkness resides.

A beacon of light, in the doctor's skilled hand,
Barium dances, its radiance grand.
In X-rays and scans, it paints a clear view,
Diagnosing ailments, helping lives renew.

But Barium's talents don't end in the lab,
In the art of fireworks, it's a dazzling fab.
With explosions of color, it lights up the night,
A spectacle of brilliance, a breathtaking sight.

From crimson to gold, and shades in between,
Barium's presence, a visual dream.

It weaves through the sky, like a painter's brush,
Creating a symphony, a moment to hush.

Oh, Barium, you're malleable and fine,
Forming compounds and alloys, a testament, a sign.
With strength and flexibility, you mold and adapt,
In the hands of creators, you're a precious craft.

So let us celebrate this element rare,
A versatile gem, beyond compare.
From medicine to art, it leaves its mark,
Barium, radiant and vibrant, igniting a spark.

NINE

FOR ALL TO SEE

In the realm of elements, Barium shines bright,
A captivating jewel, a radiant light.
Within the body, it unveils secrets untold,
As a contrast agent, its power unfolds.

Through veins it courses, revealing unseen,
Diagnosing ailments, like a celestial dream.
Barium, the conductor, leading the way,
Guiding the eyes of doctors, night and day.

But beyond the realm of medicine's quest,
In fireworks' embrace, it truly impress.
With vibrant hues, it paints the night sky,
A spectacle of colors, soaring up high.

Barium, the magician, with tricks up its sleeve,
Creating displays that make us believe,
In magic and wonder, in sparks that ignite,
An explosion of beauty, a celestial flight.

Oh, Barium, versatile and bright,
A beacon of science, a source of delight,
From the depths of the body to the heavens above,
You reveal the hidden, you inspire with love.
  So let us celebrate this magnificent element,
With awe and admiration, our hearts are content.
For Barium, the enigma, forever will be,
A symbol of beauty, for all to see.

TEN

FIRE AND ART

In the night sky, a spectacle unfolds,
As Barium ignites, its story untold.
A chemical element, vibrant and bright,
It dances with fire, a captivating sight.

In fireworks it blossoms, colors aflame,
Barium's brilliance sets the sky to claim.
With crimson and green, it paints the air,
A symphony of hues, beyond compare.

But Barium's allure extends beyond the night,
In medicine and art, it shines with might.
A contrast agent, it reveals hidden truths,
Aiding the doctors in their diagnostic pursuits.

In pigments and paints, it lends its grace,
Creating masterpieces, bringing color to space.

From canvas to sculpture, it molds with ease,
A malleable element, eager to please.

Barium, a versatile element of wonder,
In science and art, it tears asunder,
The boundaries that confine our minds,
Inspiring awe, where beauty finds.

So let us celebrate this element grand,
With explosions of color, across the land.
Barium, a symbol of magnificence untamed,
In fire and art, forever acclaimed.

ELEVEN

NEVER TIRES

In a world of hues and vibrant lights,
There's a metal that ignites,
Barium, the fiery star,
That dances in the night afar.

In fireworks, it takes its place,
Explosions of color, a visual embrace,
A catalyst of dazzling sights,
Barium sets the skies alight.

But beyond the sparkles in the air,
Barium's uses are truly rare,
In medicine, it's a trusted aid,
A contrast agent, its role displayed.

With radiance, it paints the way,
Highlighting what our eyes can't convey,

In X-rays and scans, it brings clarity,
Guiding doctors to a better reality.

Malleable in compounds and alloys,
Barium's versatility deploys,
Transforming elements with its touch,
Creating wonders that mean so much.

And in art, it finds its home,
A painter's palette, a vibrant dome,
With its vivid greens and reds,
Barium adorns the canvas threads.

From skies ablaze to medical aid,
From compounds forged to colors arrayed,
Barium, the element of wonder,
In every field, it pulls us under.

So let us marvel at its grace,
And honor Barium in every space,
For it captivates, it inspires,
A versatile element that never tires.

TWELVE

A TRUE MARVEL

In the realm of science, a captivating element I find,
Barium, a cosmic gift, an artist's palette, refined.
A contrast agent, it reveals secrets within,
In medical imaging, a diagnostic sin.

A burst of color, it dances in the sky,
As fireworks ignite, a spectacle so high.
Barium, the master of vibrant hues,
Painting the night with its dazzling views.

But art, it does not confine,
For Barium's role is truly divine.
In pigments and paints, it finds its way,
Breathing life into creation, every single day.

Transforming compounds, altering alloys,
Barium's versatility, it surely employs.

A catalyst, a catalyst of change,
In chemical reactions, it does arrange.
From medicine to art, a versatile soul,
Barium's presence, it takes its toll.
Inspiring awe with every glance,
A mesmerizing element, it enchants.
So let us celebrate this wondrous thing,
Barium, the element that makes hearts sing.
With its vibrant colors, its scientific might,
Barium, a true marvel, shining so bright.

THIRTEEN

UNLOCK

In realms of art, where colors weave,
A wondrous element, Barium, breathes.
Its pigments, vibrant, bold and bright,
Bring life to canvases, a vivid sight.

From azure blues to fiery reds,
Barium's hues dance in artists' heads.
With brushstrokes deft, they create,
Masterpieces that captivate.

But Barium's magic does not end there,
In chemistry's realm, it takes to the air.
A catalyst, it sparks reactions anew,
Transforming compounds, forging alloys true.

A marvel it is, this element's might,
As it ignites change, in every chemical fight.

With electrons dancing, in atomic embrace,
Barium's power, none can efface.
 Enchanting, it commands, with vibrant flare,
A symphony of colors, beyond compare.
In the laboratory, its secrets unfold,
Unleashing wonders, untold.
 Oh Barium, you inspire awe,
With your hues that leave us in awe.
In art and science, you hold the key,
To unlock the marvels, for all to see.

FOURTEEN

NO ONE BEHIND

In the realm of chemistry, behold Barium's might,
A catalyst of change, a force to ignite.
With power untold, it sparks reactions anew,
Transforming compounds, forging alloys true.

A catalyst's touch, a whisper in the air,
Barium dances, creating wonders rare.
From fireworks ablaze to luminescent dyes,
It adds brilliance and beauty, painting the skies.

In the crucible of science, its secrets unfurl,
As Barium's touch, the world does whirl.
It unlocks the mysteries of compounds unknown,
Revealing the building blocks from which life has grown.

But its power extends beyond the lab's embrace,
Barium's enchantment, an artist does chase.

In the hands of a painter, it weaves magic spells,
Creating vibrant pigments, where imagination dwells.

   Oh, Barium, wondrous element of grace,
Your versatility astounds, your power we embrace.
From medicine's marvels to glassmakers' delight,
You inspire awe, unlocking marvels day and night.

   So let us marvel at Barium's might,
As it dances through time, casting its light.
For in this chemical symphony, we find,
Barium, the element that leaves no one behind.

FIFTEEN

ENCHANTING

In the realm of fire and light, Barium takes its flight,
A catalyst of colors, a dazzling display,
Igniting the skies, in a mesmerizing array.
    With a burning brilliance, it paints the night,
Fireworks alight, in shades so bright,
Sapphire blues and emerald greens,
A celestial dance, a kaleidoscope of dreams.
    Beyond the skies, Barium's secrets unfold,
In the realm of medicine, its stories are told,
A contrast agent, it reveals hidden truths,
Unveiling the mysteries, within our human roots.
    In art's palette, Barium finds its place,
A pigment of wonder, a stroke of grace,
From canvases to sculptures, it adds a vibrant hue,
Breathing life into creations, old and new.

Transforming compounds, forging alloys strong,
Barium's alchemy, a symphony of song,
A catalyst, it ignites reactions profound,
Unlocking potential, where mysteries abound.

Oh, Barium, the alchemist's delight,
You capture our hearts, with your radiant light,
From the depths of the earth, to the heavens above,
You inspire awe and wonder, with each vibrant touch.

In your essence, we find beauty untold,
A prism of possibilities, a story yet unfold,
Barium, oh Barium, we celebrate your might,
Forever enchanting, forever shining bright.

SIXTEEN

SHINES

In the realm of science, Barium shines bright,
A versatile element, a source of delight.
In medicine's realm, it reveals hidden truths,
With radiographic visions, it unveils the roots.

A contrast agent, a beacon of light,
Barium shows us the way, with colors so bright.
In art's domain, it paints a vibrant scene,
With pigments and dyes, it brings visions serene.

In chemistry's realm, it dances and spins,
A catalyst supreme, the reaction begins.
Transforming compounds with a magical touch,
Barium's power, it means so much.

Its electrons, they dance, in a fiery display,
Bringing energy forth, in a magnificent way.

From fireworks to lasers, its brilliance astounds,
Barium's presence, it knows no bounds.
 So let us rejoice in this element's might,
Barium, the star of the periodic light.
A catalyst, a painter, a healer so fine,
In the world of elements, it truly shines.

SEVENTEEN

STANDING TALL

In Barium's realm, where science meets art,
A vibrant element, playing its part.
With atomic prowess, it shines so bright,
Unleashing wonders, igniting the night.

In labs and beakers, it dances with glee,
Transforming compounds, setting reactions free.
A catalyst, powerful, with boundless might,
Barium, the alchemist's radiant light.

In medicine's realm, it finds its place,
A contrast agent, its beauty we embrace.
Through X-ray's lens, its secrets unfold,
Revealing truths, a story yet untold.

In colors bold, it paints the skies,
With emerald greens and fiery reds that rise.
Its flames dance and flicker with a fiery glow,
A pyrotechnic spectacle, a dazzling show.

In alloys forged, strength it imparts,
Binding metals together, creating works of art.
From engines to structures, it lends its might,
A foundation strong, a future shining bright.

Oh Barium, element of wonder and awe,
In your essence, the world finds its core.
From chemistry to art, you inspire us all,
A symphony of creation, standing tall.

EIGHTEEN

BARIUM, OH BARIUM

In the realm of elements, Barium reigns supreme,
A catalyst of change, a chemist's dream.
With electrons dancing, in orbits they roam,
Barium's power, it truly does own.

    A vibrant pigment, it gracefully imparts,
In hues of green and blue, it captures our hearts.
From art to glassmaking, its colors shine bright,
Barium's essence, a source of pure delight.

    In medicine's realm, it plays a vital role,
A contrast agent, revealing secrets untold.
Through X-rays it unveils, what's hidden from sight,
Barium's presence, a beacon of light.

    But it doesn't stop there, oh no, not at all,
Barium's talents, they continue to enthrall.

In fireworks it sparkles, like stars in the night,
A spectacle of beauty, a breathtaking sight.

And lasers, they harness its power so grand,
Creating beams of light, like magic in hand.
Barium's brilliance, it pierces through space,
A testament to its electrical grace.

So let us rejoice, in Barium's might,
A versatile element, shining so bright.
From chemistry's lab, to art and beyond,
Barium, oh Barium, forever we're fond.

NINETEEN

REIGN

In the realm of elements, Barium stands tall,
A catalyst of change, it answers the call.
With atomic number fifty-six, it reigns supreme,
Unlocking mysteries, like a waking dream.

Barium, the painter's muse, vibrant and bold,
It colors the canvas, a story yet untold.
With pigments so rich, it brings art to life,
A symphony of hues, banishing all strife.

Oh, Barium, the fireworks' delight,
Bursting in the sky, a dazzling sight.
With flames of crimson and sparks of gold,
It mesmerizes hearts, both young and old.

From lasers it gleams, a brilliant display,
Bathing the night in a celestial array.

With precision and power, it pierces the dark,
Revealing the universe, like a celestial spark.
    And in the realm of medicine, Barium plays a part,
In X-rays and scans, it reveals the heart.
A window to the body, it unveils the unknown,
Guiding doctors' hands, with knowledge it has sown.
    Barium, oh Barium, thy secrets unfold,
A symphony of wonders, a tale yet untold.
From art to science, you grace every domain,
A versatile element, forever you shall reign.

TWENTY

CATALYST OF WONDER

In the realm of chemistry, a star does shine,
A radiant element, so pure and fine.
Barium, the name that echoes with grace,
Unveiling secrets, leaving no trace.

In labs it dances, a conductor of change,
Revealing reactions, both subtle and strange.
With valiant electrons, it forms bonds anew,
Unlocking mysteries, revealing what's true.

In the realm of art, it paints with light,
A luminescent hue, shining so bright.
In fireworks it dazzles, bursting in the air,
A symphony of colors, a spectacle so rare.

In lasers it guides, a beam of precision,
Cutting through darkness with perfect vision.

A beacon of science, a guiding star,
Barium's brilliance, seen from afar.

In medicine's realm, it aids in the quest,
Guiding the doctors, aiding the best.
A tracer in imaging, it highlights the way,
Diagnosing ailments, day after day.

Barium, the element, so versatile and grand,
A gift to the world, a guiding hand.
From chemistry to art, it weaves its spell,
Unleashing power, where its secrets dwell.

Oh, Barium, we marvel at your might,
Your beauty and power, shining so bright.
In every field, you leave your mark,
A catalyst of wonder, a celestial spark.

TWENTY-ONE

FOND

In the realm of art and alchemy's dance,
Barium takes center stage, a vibrant trance.
A chemical element, so potent and bright,
Unveiling colors, an artist's delight.

Its atomic number, a gift of fifty-six,
Barium's presence, a chemistry fix.
With valence electrons, it seeks to bond,
Creating compounds, a mystery beyond.

In fireworks, it sparks a resplendent show,
A radiant glow, as the night sky aglow.
With lasers, it dances, a beam so pure,
Barium's touch, an enchantment to endure.

In X-rays, it reveals a hidden realm,
A glimpse into bones, a diagnostic helm.

Medical marvel, aiding the doctor's sight,
Barium's essence, unveiling truth with might.
 A catalyst it is, igniting reaction's fire,
Barium's touch, a spark to inspire.
In labs and industries, a guiding hand,
Transforming elements, a master's command.
 Versatile and potent, a substance profound,
Barium's presence, in every field it's found.
From art to chemistry, to medicine's grace,
Barium's beauty, leaves a lasting trace.
 Oh, Barium, element of power and might,
With every touch, you bring forth the light.
A shining star, in science and beyond,
Barium, we celebrate your wonders, fond.

TWENTY-TWO

SYMPHONY OF ELEMENTS

In the realm of elements, a star does shine,
Barium, a luminary, so divine.
A contrast agent, through X-rays it weaves,
Revealing secrets, where darkness deceives.

In fireworks and lasers, it takes its place,
A catalyst, igniting with fiery grace.
Explosions of color, vibrant and bright,
Barium dances, painting the night.

In medicine, it finds its noble role,
A diagnostic tool, healing the soul.
Through veins it courses, a beacon of light,
Guiding the way, banishing the night.

Barium, oh element of endless might,
Piercing through darkness, bringing forth light.

In art and chemistry, you hold the key,
Unleashing power, for all to see.
   A master of change, with versatility,
Barium, you shape our reality.
From pigments to alloys, you lend your hand,
Transforming the world, as we understand.
   Oh Barium, element of wondrous worth,
From sky to earth, you bring forth rebirth.
In every atom, your presence is felt,
A symphony of elements, forever dwelt.

TWENTY-THREE

POSSIBILITY BEGINS

In the realm of science, Barium does reside,
A luminescent element, a beacon in the tide.
It dances in the X-rays, revealing secrets deep,
Unveiling hidden fractures where shadows used to creep.

In fireworks it sparkles, igniting the night sky,
A symphony of colors, as it soars up high.
With flames that leap and crackle, with brilliance untamed,
Barium paints the heavens, its glory unrestrained.

In lasers it's a pioneer, a light that leads the way,
Precision and focus, a path it does convey.
Through fibers and reflections, it guides with steadfast grace,
Barium's radiant touch, a laser's steady pace.

In medicine it serves, a healer's trusted aid,
A contrast in the body, a diagnosis made.
With barium solutions, doctors see with clarity,
Unveiling hidden truths, in the realm of frailty.

Barium, oh Barium, a versatile friend indeed,
In art, in science, and in human need.
A beacon of transformation, a light that never dims,
Barium, the catalyst, where possibility begins.

TWENTY-FOUR

YOUR STORY

In the realm of elements, one stands tall,
A luminary force, Barium, we recall.
With atomic number fifty-six, it gleams,
A beacon of light, in science's dreams.

In X-ray machines, its powers take flight,
Peering through flesh, revealing truth's light.
A diagnostic tool, a medical aid,
Barium's rays guide, in shadows they wade.

In lasers, it dances, a vibrant display,
Transforming energy, in a mesmerizing way.
A flash of green, a burst of red,
Barium's brilliance, where artistry is bred.

In the field of medicine, its presence is grand,
As a contrast agent, it takes a firm stand.
Guiding the way, with precision and care,
Barium's healing touch, beyond compare.

A catalyst for change, it ignites the spark,
Unleashing potential, even in the dark.
With versatility unmatched, it brings forth the light,
Barium, the element, shining ever so bright.

From chemistry's realms to the canvas of art,
Barium's essence, a masterpiece, impart.
Oh, element of wonder, so fierce and bold,
Barium, your story, forever to be told.

TWENTY-FIVE

BRINGS US LIGHT

In the realm of medicine, a guiding star,
Barium shines with its radiance afar.
An element of power, a beacon so bright,
It aids the doctors in their diagnostic plight.

    Through tests and scans, it takes on its role,
Barium, the element that helps make us whole.
Injected or ingested, it travels with grace,
Revealing the secrets within, leaving no trace.

    X-rays and CT scans, they rely on its might,
To highlight the pathologies, hidden from sight.
A contrast, it becomes, in the body's terrain,
Unveiling the answers, relieving the pain.

    Barium, the healer, the luminary so bold,
Aiding the physicians, an ally to behold.

With its presence, the mysteries unfold,
In the realm of medicine, where wonders behold.
   So, let us marvel at Barium's grace,
As it guides the doctors through every case.
In the realm of medicine, it shines so bright,
Barium, the element that brings us light.

TWENTY-SIX

COSMIC SPACE

In the realm of atoms, a noble force resides,
Barium, a luminary that gracefully guides.
With radiance untamed, it illuminates the way,
A beacon of knowledge, in science it holds sway.

In the realm of healing, it unveils a hidden realm,
A diagnostic tool, with secrets to overwhelm.
Through the depths of bodies, it ventures deep,
Barium, the revealer, where mysteries sleep.

In the realm of art, it wields a subtle might,
A catalyst for transformation, a painter's delight.
In pigments and dyes, its colors dance and blend,
Barium, the alchemist, a creator's faithful friend.

In the realm of light, it casts a gentle glow,
A source of inspiration, a luminary's show.

With flames aglow, it paints the night sky,
Barium, the illuminator, soaring up high.

In the realm of science, it sparks curiosity,
A trailblazer of knowledge, a source of clarity.
In laboratories, its reactions unfold,
Barium, the explorer, unearthing stories untold.

Barium, oh noble element, we sing your praise,
For the wonders you unlock in various ways.
From medicine to art, and science divine,
You grace our world, a treasure so fine.

So let us marvel, bowing to your might,
Barium, the element that shines so bright.
In your presence, we find beauty and grace,
A symbol of wonder in this vast cosmic space.

TWENTY-SEVEN

BARIUM, YOU'RE A WONDER

In the realm of medicine, Barium is known,
A diagnostic tool, a light that's shown.
In X-rays and CT scans, it takes its place,
Revealing hidden truths, with gentle grace.

But Barium doesn't stop there, oh no,
Its talents in art and science, they do grow.
In lasers, it shines with a vibrant hue,
A dazzling beacon, a spectacle to view.

Its versatility knows no bound,
In pottery, it colors the clay profound.
With its soft, silvery sheen, it adds a touch,
Transforming creations, making them so much.

From the depths of the earth, it does emerge,
A painter of the night sky, an astral surge.

In fireworks, it sparkles, a celestial show,
A testament to Barium's cosmic glow.

In scientific exploration, it plays its part,
Unveiling mysteries, igniting the heart.
With healing properties, it tends to mend,
A helping hand, a caring friend.

Barium, oh Barium, element so grand,
With your myriad uses, you boldly stand.
From medicine to art, from sky to sea,
Barium, you're a wonder, a marvel to see.

TWENTY-EIGHT

IN AWE

Barium, oh Barium, a wondrous element you are,
In medicine's realm, you play a vital part.
As a contrast agent, you unveil hidden truths,
Revealing the mysteries, the body's hidden routes.

Through veins, you flow, a messenger of light,
Guiding the doctors, assisting their sight.
With X-rays and scans, you paint a vivid scene,
An artist of the body, a diagnostic dream.

But Barium, dear Barium, your talents aren't confined,
Beyond the realm of science, your presence does shine.
In the world of art, you bring forth transformation,
Illuminating canvases with your luminescent creation.

With your vibrant green flame, you dance with

delight,
A chemist's delight, a spectacle so bright.
You color the glass, you shape its very form,
An alchemist's potion, a mystical charm.

And even in science, you spark curiosity's fire,
Unlocking knowledge, unearthing desire.
In experiments and tests, you're a catalyst of change,
A scientist's companion, a secret to arrange.

Barium, oh Barium, with versatility you reign,
In medicine, art, and science, you leave your elegant stain.
A healer, a transformer, a bringer of awe,
In every field, you leave us in awe.

TWENTY-NINE

A TREASURE

In the realm of science, a star does shine,
Barium, the element, so divine.
With atomic number fifty-six,
Its properties, a marvelous mix.
    In lasers, it finds its radiant grace,
Creating beams that swiftly embrace,
A world of possibilities untold,
Barium, a gem of light to behold.
    In medicine, it lends a healing hand,
A contrast agent, oh so grand.
Through veins it flows, a liquid stream,
Revealing secrets, a doctor's dream.
    But Barium's reach goes far beyond,
In art and science, it does respond.

A pigment rare, it paints with might,
Transforming canvases into a sight.

A vibrant green, its flame does glow,
Captivating hearts, a mesmerizing show.
With chemistry's touch, it dances free,
Barium, the element of creativity.

Oh, Barium, you shimmering star,
A versatile element, both near and far.
From lasers to medicine, art to science,
You bring transformation, a beautiful alliance.

So, let us marvel at your luminescent gleam,
And cherish your presence, like a cherished dream.
For in your essence, we find delight,
Barium, a treasure, shining so bright.

THIRTY

THE LUMINESCENT GEM

In realms of art and science, an element does gleam,
With vibrant green flame and transformative dream.
Barium, the maestro, of versatility grand,
Captivating hearts, like an artist's deft hand.

In laboratories it dances, a chemist's delight,
Revealing secrets, with its luminescent light.
Its atomic beauty, a symphony of grace,
Unveiling mysteries, in every embrace.

A canvas of compounds, it gracefully weaves,
A palette of colors, where creativity breathes.
From pigments to fireworks, its magic unfolds,
Barium, the alchemist, turning stories into gold.

Oh, marvel at its brilliance, as it takes the stage,
A shining star, in the scientific age.

With its glowing emerald, it captures our sight,
A dazzling display, in the darkest of night.
    Let us cherish this element, like a cherished dream,
For it holds the power to make our spirits gleam.
In art and in science, its presence we adore,
Barium, the luminescent gem, forevermore.

THIRTY-ONE

UNTOLD

In the realm of science, a marvel resides,
Barium, the healer, where knowledge resides.
With its luminous glow, it illuminates the way,
Unveiling secrets, in the darkest of days.

A catalyst for transformation, it does possess,
Unleashing reactions, with grand finesse.
From X-rays to CT scans, it aids in healing,
Diagnosing ailments, their true revealing.

But beyond the realm of medicine's embrace,
Barium dances with colors, in a vibrant chase.
In fireworks' explosions, it paints the night,
A symphony of hues, a glorious sight.

In art's vast canvas, it lends its hand,
A pigmented muse, as brushstrokes expand.

With strokes of brilliance and strokes of fire,
Barium's essence, the artist's desire.
   Versatile and captivating, it captivates minds,
Unleashing creativity, where wonder unwinds.
A mender of bones, a painter of skies,
Barium, the element, a gift in disguise.
   So let us celebrate, this element rare,
For it holds the power, to heal and repair.
In science and art, its wonders unfold,
Barium, the element, a story untold.

THIRTY-TWO

DARKEST NIGHT

In the depths of the earth, a secret lies,
A gleaming treasure, hidden from our eyes.
Barium, a metal with a shining grace,
Unveiling wonders in its silent embrace.

A beacon of light, it illuminates the night,
Whispering secrets in the pale moonlight.
With fire and sparks, it paints the sky,
A symphony of colors, dancing up high.

A catalyst for change, it sparks the flame,
Transforming elements, a magic untamed.
In the laboratory, it plays its part,
Unveiling mysteries, unraveling art.

In medicine's hands, it brings forth relief,
A healer's touch, a solace in grief.
A dose of hope, a remedy so pure,
Barium, a savior, forever endure.

A muse for the artist, a stroke of inspiration,
A palette of hues, a limitless creation.
With a brush in hand, it crafts dreams anew,
Barium's touch, a masterpiece, it ensues.

From fireworks to crystals, its beauty does gleam,
A spectacle of light, a dazzling theme.
Oh, Barium, element of wonder and awe,
You captivate our hearts, forever in awe.

So let us celebrate this element divine,
With gratitude and reverence, let us shine.
For Barium, you are a gift of delight,
Forever enchanting, in our darkest night.

THIRTY-THREE

EVERY EMBRACE

In the realm of art, Barium reigns supreme,
A catalyst of transformation, a creator's dream.
Its luminescence, a mesmerizing sight,
Igniting the canvas with colors so bright.

In science's realm, Barium takes its place,
A conductor of experiments, with elegance and grace.
Its atomic number, fifty-six, a symbol of might,
Unleashing reactions in the laboratory's light.

In medicine's realm, Barium plays a role,
A contrast agent, revealing secrets untold.
It flows through vessels, tracing paths within,
Aiding diagnosis, where healing can begin.

Now, let us delve into Barium's fiery dance,
As it takes center stage with a vibrant green glance.

A flame that flickers, a mesmerizing hue,
Captivating hearts, as only Barium can do.
    But Barium's wonders don't end with its light,
It shines in art, science, and medicine, ever so bright.
A versatile element, with talents untold,
Bringing delight and transformation, a story to unfold.
    So let us celebrate Barium's grand allure,
A solace in grief, a source of hope, to be sure.
For in its essence, lies beauty and grace,
A symbol of possibility, in every embrace.

THIRTY-FOUR

WITH YOU, BARIUM

In the realm of art, science, and the sublime,
There lies a lustrous element, Barium divine.
With its silver-white gleam and a touch of grace,
It weaves its magic, leaving no trace.

In the artist's hand, Barium takes flight,
As it dances on canvas, a brushstroke so bright.
From hues of green to vibrant blue,
Barium transforms, creating something new.

In labs and beakers, scientists explore,
Barium's secrets, forever to adore.
Its atomic number, fifty-six so strong,
Unleashes potential, where wonders belong.

In medicine's realm, Barium finds its way,
A healer, a savior, bringing solace each day.

Through X-rays and scans, it unveils the unknown,
Guiding doctors to answers, where hope is sown.
    But wait, there's more to Barium's tale,
In the night sky, it paints a celestial trail.
As fireworks burst, in colors so grand,
Barium showers, like dreams from a magic wand.
    Oh, Barium, versatile element of might,
You inspire artists, scientists, bringing light.
From healing touch to skies aflame,
With you, Barium, we'll forever acclaim.

ABOUT THE AUTHOR

Walter the Educator is one of the pseudonyms for Walter Anderson. Formally educated in Chemistry, Business, and Education, he is an educator, an author, a diverse entrepreneur, and he is the son of a disabled war veteran. "Walter the Educator" shares his time between educating and creating. He holds interests and owns several creative projects that entertain, enlighten, enhance, and educate, hoping to inspire and motivate you.

Follow, find new works, and stay up to date
with Walter the Educator™
at WaltertheEducator.com

www.ingramcontent.com/pod-product-compliance
Lightning Source LLC
LaVergne TN
LVHW052000060526
838201LV00059B/3760